Churches of the Yorkshire Wolds (2)

by Christine R. Barker

with photographs by John R. Crossland

Hutton Press 1985

Phototypeset in 11 on 12 pt Times Roman
and printed by The Walkergate Press Ltd.,
Lewis House, Springfield Way, Anlaby, Hull HU10 6RX

Copyright © 1985
Hutton Press Ltd.,
130 Canada Drive, Cherry Burton, Beverley
North Humberside HU17 7SB

ISBN 0 907033 29 6

FOR MY MOTHER

ACKNOWLEDGEMENTS

I should like to express my thanks to the Vicars of all the Churches for supplying me with information and advice, and particularly to the following: Major Donald Duke, MBE, Churchwarden and Treasurer of All Saints, Nafferton; Rev. David Hawkins, Rector of Burton Agnes with Harpham; Rev. Jack Reed, Vicar of Rudston and Boynton, and his Churchwardens; Rev. Father John R. Meeres, Vicar of Langtoft; Rev. P. H. F. Scott, Vicar of Sledmere, Fridaythorpe and Fimber; Rev. C. I. McN. Smith, Vicar of Kirby Grindalythe; Rev. William F. J. Everitt, former Vicar of Wharram-le-Street; Mrs. Irene Megginson, Secretary of Bishop Wilton P.C.C.; and the Rev. J. Woodhouse, Team Rector of Pocklington, all of whom made very helpful comments on the various stages of my manuscript.

    My special thanks are also due to the Rev. Jonathan Eades, Anglican Chaplain to the University of Dundee, for his invaluable assistance with the final draft of the text; to Marilyn White for her drawing of the map of the area; and last, but by no means least, to John Crossland for taking all the photographs.

C. R. Barker,
May, 1985

CONTENTS

	Page
Introduction	6
Nafferton, All Saints	8
Harpham, St. John of Beverley	10
Burton Agnes, St. Martin	13
Boynton, St. Andrew	17
Rudston, All Saints	20
Thwing, All Saints	24
Langtoft, St. Peter	26
Sledmere, St. Mary	29
Kirby Grindalythe, St. Andrew	31
Wharram-le-Street, St. Mary	34
Wharram Percy, St. Martin	36
Fimber, St. Mary	39
Fridaythorpe, St. Mary	41
Bishop Wilton, St. Edith	44
Pocklington, All Saints	45
Glossary	48
Bibliography	49

LIST OF ILLUSTRATIONS

	Page
St. Mary's, Sledmere	Cover
Map of the area	7
All Saints, Nafferton	9
St. John of Beverley's, Harpham	11
St. Martin's, Burton Agnes	15
St. Andrew's, Boynton	18
All Saints, Rudston, and the Monolith	23
All Saints, Thwing	25
St. Peter's, Langtoft	27
Norman font from Cottam, now at Langtoft	28
St. Andrew's, Kirby Grindalythe	33
St. Mary's, Wharram-le-Street	34
West doorway, Wharram-le-Street	35
St. Martin's, Wharram Percy	37
St. Mary's, Fimber	40
St. Mary's, Fridaythorpe	42
The clock at St. Mary's, Fridaythorpe	43
St. Edith's, Bishop Wilton	44
All Saints, Pocklington	46

Introduction

The first volume of CHURCHES OF THE WOLDS presented a brief 'tour' of fourteen churches in an area to the south-west of Driffield, the intention being that the churches could be visited in a round trip. This second volume follows a similar pattern, beginning at Nafferton and ending at Pocklington, taking in fifteen churches in a slighty more northerly area of the Yorkshire Wolds.

This tour is longer than that in Volume 1, and it is not really possible to view all the churches in one day – although John Crossland, who took the photographs, did manage to get round all fifteen churches one fine summer's day.

The splendour and size of many of the churches in what is now a fairly sparsely populated area of the Wolds may seem surprising to us today, but in the Middle Ages the East Riding, with its good farming land, was more densely populated than the rest of Yorkshire since large numbers of labourers were employed on each farm. Although some of the villages are now quite tiny and their churches often difficult to find, they retain considerable charm and are well worth a visit.

The historical interest in this part of Yorkshire is immeasurable. Wharram Percy is one of the East Riding's most famous deserted villages and is still being excavated; the church at nearby Wharram-le-Street is the oldest church on the Wolds, dating from early Saxon days; the tiny village of Harpham, near Nafferton, is famous as the birthplace of St. John of Beverley, and Rudston can boast not only the tallest standing stone in Britain (close by the church) but also the grave of the writer Winifred Holtby, who was born in Rudston in 1898. Kirby Grindalythe's church has a splendid and unique mosaic on the west wall of the nave; Bishop Wilton has a beautiful mosaic floor copied from one in the Vatican; and both Burton Agnes and Sledmere have magnificent stately homes which should, if possible, be viewed along with their churches.

Sledmere House is, of course, the home of the Sykes family who have played such a large part in the history of the East Riding and its churches. The vital role of Sir Tatton Sykes (d.1913), continuing the work begun by his father, was noted in Volume 1, and his efforts are even more in evidence in the churches included in the present volume. As a token of his invaluable contribution to the ecclesiastical heritage of the East Riding, a bust of Sir Tatton is displayed in all the churches he restored (though more prominently in some churches than others).

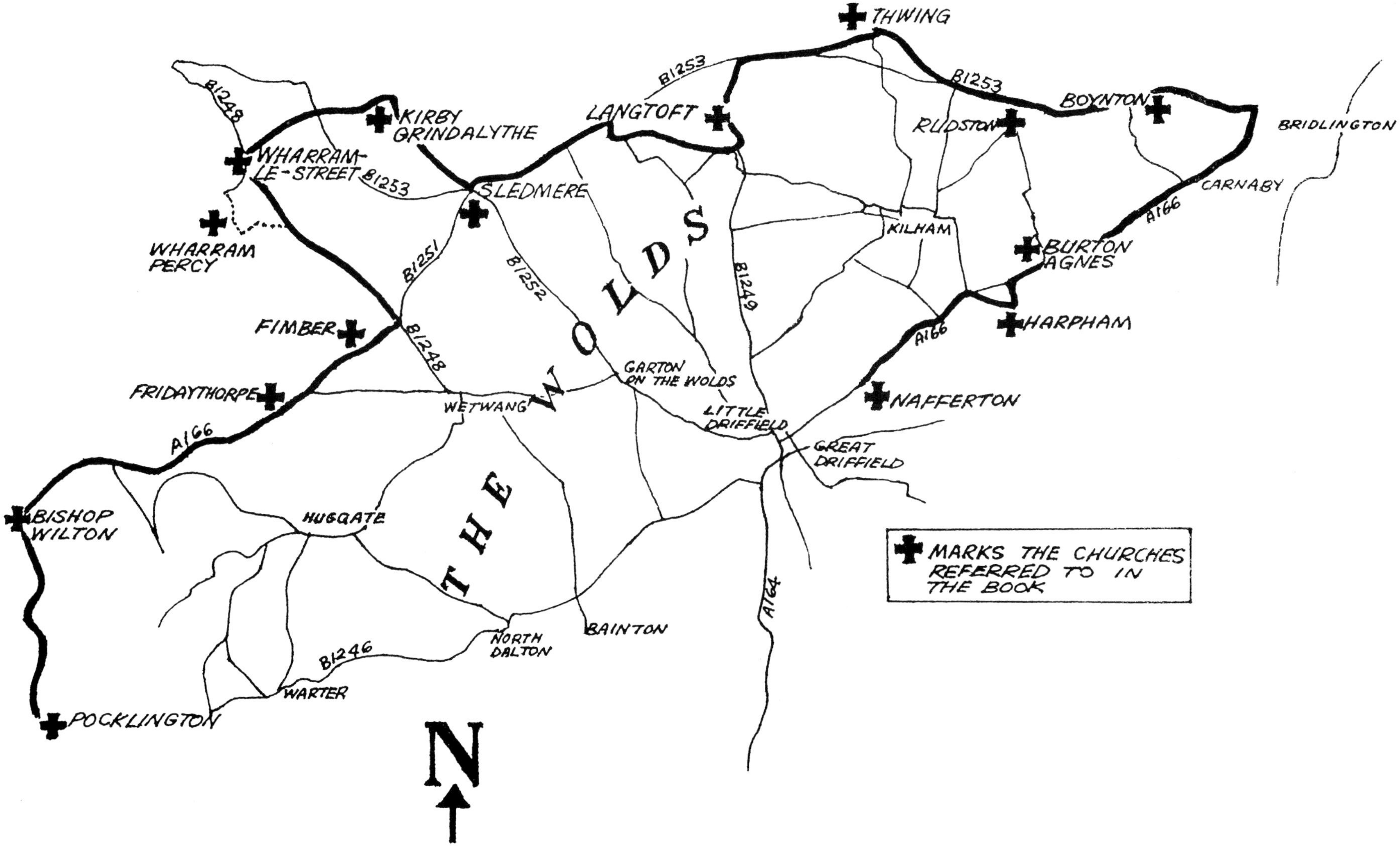
THWING
B1253
B1248
KIRBY GRINDALYTHE
LANGTOFT
RUDSTON
BOYNTON
BRIDLINGTON
WHARRAM-LE-STREET
B1253
SLEDMERE
CARNABY
A166
WHARRAM PERCY
KILHAM
BURTON AGNES
B1251
B1252
THE WOLDS
B1249
HARPHAM
FIMBER
B1248
A166
GARTON ON THE WOLDS
FRIDAYTHORPE
NAFFERTON
WETWANG
LITTLE DRIFFIELD
A166
GREAT DRIFFIELD
BISHOP WILTON
HUGGATE
MARKS THE CHURCHES REFERRED TO IN THE BOOK
A164
BAINTON
NORTH DALTON
B1246
WARTER
POCKLINGTON
N

Nafferton
All Saints

The large village of Nafferton lies a couple of miles to the north-east of Driffield, just south of the A166 road to Bridlington. In the Domesday Book the village is called Nadfartone, thereby revealing its Scandinavian origins. Nadfar was a personal name among the Norsemen, but who this particular Nadfar was and what part he played in Nafferton's history remains a mystery.

During the reign of Edward the Confessor, in the middle of the eleventh century, Nafferton was held by two Scandinavians named Bark and Karle, and was valued at £8. A pre-Conquest cemetery has been found to the north of the church.

The probable founder of the church was William de Percy (1030–1096) of the celebrated Northumbrian Percy family, who held Nafferton manor in 1086. A subsequent member of the same family, Sir Henry Percy, the 8th Baron of Alnwick, gave the church to the abbot of Meaux in 1304.

The church of All Saints, with its fine Perpendicular tower, dominates the western end of the village from its high bank, and is reached by a winding road which passes through the centre of Nafferton. Opposite the church is a large mere with a substantial population of ducks, on the other side of which is Nafferton Maltings, an impressive five-storey building which is a combined malting and watermill dating from 1840.

Most of the church is mediaeval, although the circular font, crudely carved with a lattice pattern and a top band of loops, is Norman, as is the rather odd, restored chancel arch which dates – originally – from the close of the twelfth century. The arch is pointed, but has non-matching Norman capitals. In the south wall of the chancel arch is a large, partly blocked squint with a shouldered head on the nave side and a pointed arch on the chancel side.

Above the squint on the east wall of the nave is a tablet to 'Margaret, the much revered relict of John Gregson of Appleby in Westmorland' who died in 1787, and also to the Rev. Thomas Bowness, a vicar of Nafferton, who died in 1788 and who was married to Elizabeth, only daughter of the above John and Margaret Gregson. She erected the monument 'to his manifold virtues'.

The chancel, along with the south aisle and its four-bay arcade, is fourteenth-century (Decorated), while the south aisle dates from the fifteenth century. The north arcade and clerestory are fifteenth-century Perpendicular, as is the embattled west tower.

Built into the north aisle wall is the quaint stone figure of a boy wearing a short tunic. He has crossed legs and one hand behind him, his head on a pillow. Although now in an upright position, he was presumably originally intended to be recumbent. The figure is thought to date from the thirteenth century – probably around 1250 – and is most likely the effigy of a 'Boy Bishop'. It was the custom for the young people to choose a leader, who held this position from Christmas to Epiphany. If he died during his period of office, a memorial figure was placed in the church.

On the floor in the east corner of the north aisle are two larger, recumbent stone figures which have been brought in from the churchyard. These are the canopied effigies of a man and a woman, with only the busts and lower parts of the legs visible. The rest of the figures disappears into heavy foliage tracery, now rather weather-worn, as for centuries the slabs lay in the open on the south side of the church. The canopies above the heads of the figures are also rather mutilated. Nothing is known about them, except that they probably date from the fourteenth century.

On the north chancel wall is a memorial to Ann Esh, who died in 1762 at the age of ten. According to her inscription 'She was bless'd, with such a happy Talent for Learning, that at four Years of Age, she was capable, punctually to read a Chapter in

9

the Bible' (i.e. with the correct expression). On the opposite wall is a tablet to Richard Esh, Gentleman, who died in 1765 at the age of fifty-three.

The church has a lovely, four-light east window with attractive tracery in its upper part. The window is signed by Wailes and is dated 1854. The stained glass is a memorial to Richard Dickson and was erected by his nephew, John Dickson, who also presented the long altar and colourfully decorated reredos. There is also a window to John Dickson himself (who died in 1899) in the south wall of the sanctuary. This is the same shape as the east window and depicts the Good Shepherd.

In 1870 the clerestory and some other windows were re-glazed and a new window installed in the south wall of the chancel. There is also some attractive twentieth-century glass in the north aisle wall. The window nearest the tower, in the part of the church used for the Sunday school, is in memory of Muriel Mary Senior (1901 – 1979), who for many years was a Sunday school teacher here.

The church's box pews date from 1828. A new organ and vestry were provided in 1870, and exactly a century later the organ was reconstructed and moved to its present position under the tower.

Other recent work on the church includes the installation of an altar rail in memory of Francis Thomas Cook in 1963, the erection of the pulpit in 1972 (given by Cecilia Anne Baldwin) in memory of Thomas and Sarah Ann Redman (her parents) and the Lady Chapel, dedicated on Whit Sunday 1971 by the Archdeacon of Cleveland. The chapel was the gift of Cyril and Marjorie Redman to commemorate thirty years of happy marriage and a long association with the church (described in an illuminated manuscript on the south wall).

Among Nafferton's vicars was Francis Orpen Morris, the great bird-lover, whose book of British birds is a standard work. He was vicar here from November 1844, and then went to Nunburnholme, where he is buried.

On the external south wall, to the west of the entrance porch, is a sundial, and on the south side of the tower, a few feet from the ground, can be traced an inscription in Norman French 'DIEU TEMPLE Y ADIE ET GARDE DU ROYNE' (May God help the Church and preserve our kingdom).

Harpham
St. John of Beverley

Continuing from Nafferton along the A166 in the direction of Bridlington, the small hamlet of Harpham, lying close by the Kelk beck, is reached by taking a right turn off the main road just before Burton Agnes.

The patron saint of the church, who is buried in a tomb inside Beverley Minster, is said to have been born in Harpham in AD 640. John, successively Bishop of Hexham and York, ended his days in his own monastery at Beverley when old age compelled him to resign his episcopal charge. He died on 7th May, 721, and is still revered as a great and miraculous healer. He was canonised as St. John of Beverley in 1037, and the mediaeval Minster was built on the site of his monastery.

Each year the children of Harpham gather primroses to place on St. John's tomb for his festival in May, when a commemorative service is held in the Minster. A patronal service is also held in Harpham church every year, preceded by a procession to St. John's Well, which lies beside the low road to Burton Agnes at the east end of the village. The well has been there for many centuries, and reputedly never fails to spring even in the driest of summers. Its waters are said to possess curative properties, and local residents and visitors still bathe their feet there. Although I do not feel competent to give a verdict on the efficacy of the well's healing powers, there was

11

certainly plenty of water there when I visited it during the long period of drought in the summer of 1984.

There is another well in Harpham too, to the west of the church, known as the Drummer Boy's Well, from a legend that a drummer boy fell into it when some soldiers were practising archery. For centuries it was believed that the boy could be heard beating his drum whenever a St. Quintin – the owners of the estate at Harpham — was to die. (The family no longer own the estate, and the boy is, presumably, now able to rest in peace).

The St. Quintins held land in Holderness seven centuries ago, and Harpham itself passed from father to son without a break from the time of Edward II until the latter part of the nineteenth century. No sign of their house is now visible, but a moat which surrounded it can still be traced on the west side of the village. The family memorials in the St. Quintin chapel in the north-east corner of the church are famous, and include the finest brass in the East Riding, commemorating Thomas de St. Quintin and his wife in four-feet long figures beneath a double canopy.

The church itself has a Norman core, but seems to have been completely rebuilt in the fourteenth century. The probable founder of the church was William St. Quintin, who is buried in an alabaster tomb under an ornate arch between the chancel and the St. Quintin chapel. The tomb is dated 1349 according to the Latin inscription which reads (in English): 'Pray for the soul of Lord William St. Quintin who died in the year 1349. Also pray for the soul of (here the inscription is missing) who died in the year of our Lord 1382, in memory of her death'.

On the top of the tomb are the engraved figures of a knight in armour with a sword and dagger, and a lady in a flowing robe and draped headdress. She is thought to be Joan de Thwing, a member of the family who held the manor of Thwing. The piece of stone bearing her name has broken off and has been replaced by a blank piece. The tomb is one of only a few examples in the East Riding of portraits in alabaster.

The sides of the tomb are decorated with quatrefoils enclosing blank shields, and a crucifixion scene in the centre. The decorative canopy above the tomb ends in stone corbels depicting the head of a man at one side and the head of a woman on the other.

The north chapel houses various monuments to the St. Quintins. The walls are covered with tablets in their memory, and the windows of the chapel have the family shields in eighteenth-century stained glass by William Peckitt of York. The shields of twenty-eight successive members of the family range from 1066 to 1490.

On the floor of the chapel are two magnificent old brasses. Nearest the altar is the double brass of Thomas St. Quintin, who died a few years after the Battle of Agincourt, and his wife Agnes, who died some twenty years later. The brass is dated 1445, and as well as a double canopy has fragments of what must once have been a splendid border. Thomas is shown as a knight in armour, with a crest of feathers and a jewelled brooch. The traditional lion is at his feet. His lady is wearing an elaborate headdress and a long gown with two small dogs in its folds, both dogs wearing collars with bells.

The other, smaller brass, is of Thomas St. Quintin of Harpham who died in 1444. The abbreviated Latin inscription reads: 'Here lies Thomas St. Quintin armiger, late Lord of Harpham, who died on the 18th day of July anno domini 1444, on whose soul may the Lord have mercy, Amen'.

The chapel also houses a more modern brass to Matthew St. Quintin (1800–1876), as well as two stone coffins and the lid of one of them, on which is carved the effigy of a lady, her feet resting on a lion. Nothing is known of this figure, but the coffins must have been found when the family vault was created under the chapel.

Another St. Quintin monument is on the north wall of the sanctuary. Dedicated to Charlotte, wife of Sir William St. Quintin, who died in 1762, the tablet depicts the figure of grief incised in white marble, signed by the famous sculptor Joseph Wilton, R.A. Up to the restoration of the church in 1914 it was over the altar at the east end and was moved to its present position to make way for the east window. The monument also commemorates Sir William de St. Quintin Bart (Charlotte's father-in-law), who died 'universally lamented' in 1795 at the age of sixty-six.

At the west end of the fourteenth-century nave is an old gallery which partially hides from view the fine Gothic arch which supports the eastern wall of the tower. The tower itself is sixty-two feet high and soars above the Plain of Holderness. There are three bells, two dated 1615 and a smaller one dated 1812.

The roof of the nave was of higher pitch before 1827 when it was altered to a flat roof. In 1935 it was raised again, but to a lower pitch than before 1827. The coping for its first position can be clearly seen on the eastern wall of the tower.

The east end of the chancel was rebuilt in brick in 1827, and the chancel, chapel and tower were all restored between 1909 and 1914 by the architect Temple Moore, who retained the Georgian furnishings. The restoration was carried out at the behest of William Herbert St. Quintin, with the help of money left for the purpose by his mother, Amy Elizabeth St. Quintin. William Herbert St. Quintin is commemorated in the stained glass of the east window dating from 1935, when the restoration of the church was completed from bequests by William and his mother.

Burton Agnes
St. Martin

Burton Agnes is a pretty village on the main road between Driffield and Bridlington, just a mile or so from the crossroads to the north of Harpham. In addition to the Hall and Church, the village is characterised by attractive white cottages, a tall memorial cross, and a duck-pond. In some respects it resembles Bishop Burton, near Beverley, which was featured in Volume 1 of 'Churches of the Wolds'.

The grey stone church stands on a hillside above the road and is reached by going past the beautiful Elizabethan Hall and down a narrow lane to the west of the Hall. The lovely old rectory stands at the gate of the church, whose south door lies through a dark tunnel of overhanging yews planted some 350 years ago.

The original church was probably made of wood, but no traces of this remain. It was rebuilt in the middle of the twelfth century with an aisleless nave, a square-ended chancel, and possibly a western tower. Parts of the original walls of this church remain at the four angles of the nave and in the chancel arch, although this was subsequently altered. Under the roof, on the north face of the south arcade, some of the corbels from the old eaves cornice have been re-used.

The church has been considerably extended over the centuries. It was given to St. Mary's Abbey, York, between 1100 and 1115, and some fifty years or so later a north aisle was created when the three-bay arcade was pierced through the north wall of the nave. Although the arches themselves are pointed, their cylindrical columns with scalloped capitals resemble those of the old Manor House, dating from 1170, part of which still stands (between the Hall and the church).

The original north aisle was only about half the width of the present one, and the south aisle, which was first added in the early thirteenth century, was also much narrower than it is today. The south arcade is much lighter in design than the north arcade and has noticeably thinner columns.

In the early fourteenth century the walls of both aisles were taken down and the aisles increased in width. The north aisle was made considerably wider than the south in order to create space for the Chantry of the Blessed Virgin founded by Roger de Somerville in 1314. In 1317 Sir Roger obtained permission to transfer the body of his wife there. The chantry was endowed with 'two messuages, two oxgangs of land, 20 carts of turf yearly, and 16 acres of land in Thornholme for the support of a chaplain to say mass for his soul and for the souls of Maude his wife, Sir Marmaduke Thwing, and Peter de Brus'.

Sir Roger died in 1337, and the earliest of the church's monuments, a massive tomb decorated with quatrefoils and roses in an arched recess in the wall of the north aisle, is believed to contain his remains and those of his wife. Sir Roger was a considerable personage in his day, and was High Sheriff of Yorkshire from 1323 to 1327. On the death of his brother, Sir Philip de Somerville in 1355, Burton Agnes passed to the Griffith family, who owned the estate for three hundred years, but who seem to have resided principally at Wichnor.

Sir Walter Griffith, who died in 1481 was, however, living here in 1457, and was probably responsible for the building of the tower and the other fifteenth-century work in the church, which included the addition of the clerestory and a chapel – later destroyed – on the north side of the north aisle. On the capitals of the lofty tower arch are carved the insignia of the Griffith family.

Sir Walter Griffith has the dubious distinction of being one of the few Yorkshire knights to have fought for the Lancastrians in the Wars of the Roses. The red rose of Lancaster on the churchwardens' staves commemorates this fact. He was married to Joan Nevill, grand-daughter of Ralph Nevill, the first Earl of Westmorland (who fought with Henry V at Agincourt), and great-grand-daughter of John of Gaunt, Duke of Lancaster. It was presumably because of this family connection that Sir Walter elected to support the Lancastrian cause.

He was fortunate enough to be pardoned for the offence in 1472 by Edward IV, but evidence of his allegiance has been preserved for posterity on his alabaster tomb in the middle of the Lady Chapel. He is represented in full plate armour, wearing the SS collar which distinguished the Lancastrians from the Yorkists, who wore the familiar white rose.

At his right side is the effigy of his wife, who is also wearing the SS-style collar. Angels are at her head, and two small dogs with bells on their collars are biting the folds of her dress. Small effigies of their son and daughter used to lie at either side of them, but one was stolen by vandals in the late sixties and now only that of the son remains. He lies beside his mother, and is depicted as a knight, measuring only about twenty inches from head to foot.

On the side panels of the tomb are carvings of saints. The figures on the south are (from east to west) St. Martin (to whom the church is dedicated), a bishop, St. John the Evangelist, the Virgin Mary and Gabriel in the Annunciation, John the Baptist, and another bishop. Those on the north side are all female saints: St. Martha or Juliana, St. Agnes, St. Catherine, St. Anne teaching Mary to read, St. Margaret, St. Frideswide, and St. Sithe.

Sir Walter Griffith's second wife was Agnes Constable, sister of the 'little Sir Marmaduke' who fought at Flodden at the age of seventy, as is recorded on his brass in Flamborough church. She died in 1506, and both Lady Agnes and her son, another Sir Walter Griffith, who died in 1530, stated in their wills that they wished to be buried in the chapel at Burton Agnes church. This would be the now destroyed chapel on the north side of the north aisle – the arch is still visible from the outside.

On the north wall of the Lady Chapel is a wall monument to Sir Henry Griffith, the builder of the Hall, who died in 1620, and his wife Elizabeth Throckmorton. Sir Henry, knighted by King James at York, was High Sheriff of Yorkshire in 1606.

15

A little to the east of this monument is an extraordinary one to his son, the last Sir Henry Griffith, who fought for the King in the Civil War, surrendering to Fairfax three weeks after the Battle of Marston Moor and being heavily fined by Parliament for his activities. He died in 1654, and he and his two wives are commemorated not by the usual human effigies, but by the rather macabre monument of a row of three black coffins, one above the other, with the front part of the tomb carved to represent skulls and bones. Despite the two wives, Sir Henry died without issue, and Burton Agnes then passed to the Boynton family through his sister Frances, who had married Sir Matthew Boynton in 1613.

A somewhat more tasteful memorial remembers a vicar of Burton Agnes, Thomas Dade, who died in 1759. He is commemorated by a tablet on the wall of the south aisle, above which is a finely incised white urn on a black obelisk, by an unknown craftsman.

Around 1730 various alterations were made in the church by Sir Griffith Boynton. This work included the present box pews and the arch opening from the nave into the Boynton pew.

During a further period of vigorous restoration during the incumbency of Archdeacon Robert Wilberforce, who was rector of Burton Agnes and Archdeacon of the East Riding from 1840 to 1854, the chancel was completely rebuilt. Archdeacon Wilberforce was a son of the famous social reformer, and a bust of William Wilberforce, with his hands at prayer, can be seen on a corbel on the north wall of the sanctuary. Archdeacon Wilberforce also installed the east window in memory of his father. On leaving Burton Agnes he went for a time to Oxford, and was subsequently admitted into the Roman Catholic church in Paris. His religious leanings were thus in striking contrast to those of his father, who was a staunch Evangelical.

The Norman font, simply carved with nineteen slender columns and interlacing arches, was brought into the church from the rectory stable-yard by Archdeacon Wilberforce. The carved oak cover is a good example of modern ecclesiastical carving by the 'Mouseman', Robert Thompson of Kilburn. The lectern stool and a flower-stand in the sanctuary are further examples of his work.

There is, in fact, a great deal of fine wood carving in the church, notably the very unusual oak lectern carved with figures of the Four Evangelists round the stem. Not only do the Evangelists themselves have extremely gloomy expressions, beneath each of them there is also a carving of a grotesque face of the type generally reserved for gargoyles. The under sides of the hinged seats in the back rows of the choir stalls have misericords, each of them elaborately carved, as are the beams of the chancel roof.

The east window of the north aisle, designed by William Peckitt of York, has quaint portraits of Sir Roger de Somerville and his wife, he in armour and she in a striped mantle and draped headdress. Above the font is a very old window composed of twenty-nine ovals, each one slightly different in shape. The ovals represent eggs – a symbol of the Resurrection.

Outside, the churchyard has been cleared of its headstones – over sixty of them – which have been re-erected around its border.

The Hall and Manor House
Sir Henry Griffith (b. 1559) rebuilt Burton Agnes Hall to replace the Norman Manor House of 1170, part of which still stands. It is concealed in an Elizabethan brick casing and lies to the west of the Hall. It is one of very few of its kind left in the country and is in the care of the Department of the Environment. In a corner behind it is a donkey-wheel originally used for drawing water from the adjacent well.

The Hall itself, which was rebuilt between 1598 and 1610, is a magnificent building of mellow red brick with stone dressings. The exterior is distinguished by square bays on the east and west sides and semi-circular bays on the south front. A gatehouse with octagonal towers, built in 1610, stands at the entrance to the Hall grounds. It is four storeys high, and its four angle turrets are crowned with lead cupolas. Above its arch are the arms of James

I flanked by female figures. The house is beautifully furnished and – among many other priceless exhibits – has a number of notable French paintings by Cézanne, Pisarro, Gaugin, and Matisse.

Burton Agnes Hall also boasts one of Yorkshire's most famous ghosts. The 'screaming skull' belongs to Anne, youngest daughter of Sir Henry Griffith, the builder of the Hall. She died after being attacked by two highwaymen at Harpham, and on her deathbed made her family promise that her head should remain forever in the house she loved and whose completion she never saw.

When her sisters forgot their promise and buried her, head and all, in the churchyard, the Hall was immediately filled with ghostly disturbances, screams and groans. The coffin was opened, and Anne's head was found severed from her body. The skull was reburied in the house, and any attempt to remove it has been followed by a resumption of the ghostly manifestations with renewed vigour. It is now thought to be built into a secret hiding place in a wall of the great hall, and Anne's spirit has remained in peace ever since.

Boynton
St. Andrew

The easiest way to get to Boynton from Burton Agnes is to continue along the A166 to the outskirts of Bridlington, then follow the signs towards Rudston, which are quite clearly marked. This means travelling westwards from Bridlington until the old Roman road to York is reached, now – less romantically – the B1253. Boynton lies some three miles along this road.

The church of St. Andrew is situated at the south end of the village, close to the gates of Boynton Hall, at the end of a tree-lined lane. It is small, and looks somewhat unpromising from the outside, but has a surprising and colourful Georgian interior which is far more spacious than might be imagined from the exterior. The church is well maintained, and serves a thriving and active community.

There may have been a church in Boynton before 1066. The fact that it is dedicated to St. Andrew, like almost all the churches along the stream known as the Gypsey Race, suggests that, like the others, it was founded by St. Wilfrid in the seventh century. If this is so, the original church was probably destroyed.

We know that a church existed between 1120 and 1127, although the first recorded vicar dates from 1268. Two Chantry chapels in the church were dedicated to St. Michael and St. Lawrence, and a third chapel (dedicated to the Virgin Mary) seems to have existed in 1324, when John de Bovington (Boynton) was granted a licence by Edward II 'for a chaplain to celebrate divine service for himself and the souls of his parents and ancestors at the altar of the Blessed Virgin' in Boynton. Of this church nothing now remains except an old stone carved with a small Celtic cross which is let into the present tower wall, and a scratch dial at the south-west corner of the nave.

The tower was built in the early fifteenth century, and is more or less in its original state. There is a Perpendicular west window, giving light to the former Strickland family pew. Above that is the bell chamber. One of the two bells is dated 1705, and the other, a rare bell by John Potter of c. 1380 and inscribed + Sancta + Maria +, is thought to have been brought from elsewhere when the church was restored in the 1760's. On one of the buttresses of the tower is an old niche with a modern figure of St. Andrew, the patron saint of the church.

In the middle of the eighteenth century all of the church except the tower was destroyed by a fire. Sir George Strickland rebuilt the nave and chancel in brick between 1768 and 1770, and added a mortuary chapel for the Strickland family at the east end of the church.

18

John Carr of York was responsible for the design of the restoration, which is essentially Georgian but with certain characteristics of the Gothic revival style. The north and south windows are Gothic in style but Georgian in proportion, and have no stone tracery or stained glass. The east window, however, is of a stone Gothic design and contains stained glass by William Peckitt, with the Strickland coat-of-arms and the date 1768. At this time the first floor of the tower was opened up to serve as a Strickland family pew. Now a vestry, this is reached from the nave by a flight of stairs and is fronted by a turned wooden balustrade.

The church's most curious memorial is the famous turkey lectern, depicting 'a turkey in its pride proper'. The lectern is of modern craftsmanship, designed by Francis Johnson, who was also responsible for the font cover. The lectern was carved in the form of a turkey to commemorate the introduction of the turkey to Britain by William Strickland, who brought the first ones from South America when he commanded one of Sebastian Cabot's ships in an expedition in the early sixteenth century. The real aim of Cabot's venture was to find gold in the New World, but all they discovered was the turkey. The turkey crest and coat-of-arms beneath it were granted to William Strickland in 1550.

The font at Boynton resembles the one at Burton Agnes and is probably Norman, with a simple design of arcading in low relief. The mason appears to have miscalculated his measurements, for one arch is only half the width of the others. The font stands on a brick base, and its colourful wooden cover, painted green, red and gold, bears the motto: 'Her children arise up and call her blessed'.

Instead of the usual chancel screen, the division between nave and chancel is marked by a double row of columns surmounted by a decorated ceiling with a frieze all round. There is a plain, wrought-iron rail at floor level. This area, created during the rebuilding period of 1768–70, served as the sanctuary until a further restoration by Dr. Bilson in 1910. The altar table was formerly placed here between the two pairs of columns, but it has now been set back in the Strickland chapel.

The Strickland mortuary chapel is situated – unusually – behind the altar, and until 1910 occupied the whole of what is now the sanctuary. Flanking the east window are monuments to the family. On the left, richly painted and gilded, with a coat-of-arms and the turkey crest, is a memorial to Sir Thomas Strickland, who died in the late seventeenth century. A less elaborate piece on the right commemorates his wife Elizabeth.

There are two large eighteenth-century monuments on the north and south walls. The cenotaph on the north wall is uninscribed. It may be by William Kent, and was probably erected by Sir William Strickland, 4th Baronet, during his lifetime. It consists of a plain plinth with a Greek key frieze supporting a sarcophagus with fluted sides and top and claw feet. In the centre is a portrait medallion. The uninscribed tablet is above the sarcophagus and is capped with a broken pediment containing a blank cartouche surmounted by the turkey crest.

The monument which does commemorate Sir William and his wife faces it on the south wall and is larger and heavier. It was erected by Sir George Strickland when the church was rebuilt.

Over the pulpit is a white marble urn in memory of another member of the family, Charles Strickland, 'an amiable young man in whose heart was centred all that was dutiful, generous and exalted'. Born in 1768, he died at Gibraltar in 1795.

Boynton Hall
The Boyntons owned the manor until the mid sixteenth century, but it was the Strickland family who were responsible for the rebuilding of the present church and Hall. They have lived at the Hall for over four hundred years.

William Strickland (died 1598) began the building of the red brick Tudor Hall which is set among beeches and sycamores in the park just beyond the church. A bridle path to Carnaby runs across the park and over the Gypsey Race. The Hall, like the church, was enlarged in the eighteenth century in Georgian style by the celebrated Yorkshire architect John Carr, while alterations early in the century are thought to have been made with the assistance of Lord Burlington and William Kent.

It was another Sir William Strickland who lived in the house when Queen Henrietta Maria took refuge there during the Civil War. She landed at Bridlington from Holland on 22nd February, 1643 with arms for Charles I. Under bombardment from Parliamentary ships, the Queen took refuge first in a ditch, with bullets 'singing merrily around her', and later moved on to Boynton Hall on her way to York. She took away the family silver and gave Sir William and his wife her picture in return.

Sir William's brother, Walter Strickland, was chosen by the Long Parliament to go to Holland to protest about the help being given to Queen Henrietta Maria. He sat in several of Cromwell's parliaments, and escaped death by the skin of his teeth at The Hague, where he was endeavouring to bring about an alliance between England and Holland. He had the good fortune to be pardoned at the Restoration, living in peace until his death eleven years later. He was buried at Flamborough, and in 1936 the actual pardon he received was found in the church safe.

Among other notable members of the Strickland family are Sir Charles Strickland, said to have been the original Martin in 'Tom Brown's Schooldays'; Hugh Strickland the naturalist, born at Reighton; and Sir George Strickland, who wrote a review of agriculture and published a valuable map of Yorkshire.

Rudston
All Saints

The village of Rudston, which has been inhabited for three or four thousand years, lies in the valley of the Gypsey Race some two miles west of Boynton along the B1253.

The name 'Rudston' derives from 'rood-stone', for only a few feet from the north-east corner of the church is an impressive Bronze Age stone monolith, the Cleopatra's Needle of the Wolds. It is estimated to weigh about forty-six tons and is the tallest standing-stone in Britain, being over twenty-five feet high – three and a half feet more than the tallest stone at Stonehenge and also surpassing the tallest of the Devil's Arrows at Boroughbridge. According to an experiment conducted by Sir William Strickland in the late eighteenth century, it is probable that the stone extends for an equal distance underground.

The monolith is a single block of rough-hewn grit-stone, and as the nearest quarry seems to have been at least ten miles away, various explanations have been put forward as to how the stone reached its present position. The most colourful theory, fueled by the fact of the stone's close proximity to the church, is that the Devil, angered at the erection of a Christian building, hurled a huge stone javelin at the church to destroy it. Due to divine intervention, he missed his aim, and the stone landed in its present position.

As the church notes point out, however, it is far more likely that the order of events was reversed, and that the church was deliberately built close to the monolith in order to establish firmly for the Christian faith a site which must have been sacred to Pagan religions from prehistoric days.

Among other explanations are that the monolith was deposited at Rudston by glacial action and erected, probably in the late Neolithic period or in the Bronze Age, for some religious or ritualistic purpose.

The 'rood' part of the village's Old English name suggests that at some time the 'stan' or stone may have had a cross-head fixed to it, possibly by Anglo-Saxon missionaries in the early days of Christianity in an attempt to 'Christianise' the site.

A smaller, upright slab, about three feet high, now stands in the north-east corner of the churchyard. Its original position was a little to the east of the monolith, and it probably has some connection with it. The churchyard itself is circular, in the Pagan tradition.

The church, standing on a hill above the village, with views of the Wolds all round, was restored and partly rebuilt by G. Fowler Jones in 1861 in typical Victorian fashion.

No church at Rudston is recorded in the Domesday Survey of 1086, although there may well have been one prior to this. A church was built here soon after the Norman Conquest, probably by William Peveral, Lord of the Manor of Rudston. Of this Norman building, all that remains is a large part of the sturdy tower, with its four feet thick walls, and the circular Norman font, which is decorated with linked arches enriched with circles and octagons. Near the font, to the left of the entrance porch, is an early fourteenth-century grave slab with an elaborately carved floriated cross design in low relief.

The original entrance to the church was through a round-headed west doorway in the tower which was later blocked and a trefoiled lancet window inserted. A small, plain, circular-headed Norman arch leads from the tower to the nave. The base of the tower is now used as a vestry.

The church was enlarged in the mid thirteenth-century, when north and south aisles were added. The tall, Early English, three-bay arcades, with round pillars and capitals supporting pointed arches, were left when the aisles were later rebuilt. The east windows in the aisles are pointed and have reticulated tracery, but the other aisle windows and the clerestory windows are square-headed, with less elaborate tracery.

There are piscinas at the east end of both aisles, and the one in the north aisle has a canopy and a bowl carved in the shape of a flower. In the same aisle is a small, rectangular opening, partially blocked, which was probably a squint to an earlier, smaller chancel. At the west end of the south aisle is a holy water stoup, probably dating from the thirteenth-century.

The chancel was rebuilt in the fourteenth-century, but has a lofty pointed arch from an earlier period which reaches to the roof. The chancel contains much excellent Decorated work, notably the large, trefoiled piscina, and three sedilia with trefoiled arches and rich, leafy gables. There is also a priest's doorway. The six chancel windows all date from the restoration of 1861, and are said to be facsimilies of the originals, containing Geometric tracery.

There have been numerous alterations and repairs to the church. In 1540 Jane Constable left £1 to repair 'the body of the church'. The chancel was reported to be in a bad state of repair in 1676, and by 1700 the whole building was in a poor way. A gallery was built in 1748, probably to house the parish orchestra, which is known to have existed for many years. The church was 'thoroughly repaired' in 1829, and was given the full Victorian restoration treatment by G. Fowler Jones in 1861.

Both aisles and the south porch were rebuilt at that time, the church was re-roofed, the tower heightened, and the chancel screen removed. In 1869 the church was re-decorated by a 'Mr. Collman of London', and the highly ornate reredos of Ancaster stone, with panels of Minton tiles, was installed. The tower clock was put in, in 1882, and the enclosed, oak choir vestry at the west end of the north aisle was erected in 1938, in memory of Alice Edith Bosville Macdonald of the Isles.

The church has some notable monuments, including two brass inscriptions on the wall of the tower vestry. One commemorates Sir William Constable, of Caythorpe (d. 1527) and his wife Jane (d. 1540), although the latter date was never filled in, and the other, by Thomas Mann of York, is to Katherine (d. 1677), wife of John Constable.

There are several nineteenth-century monuments to the Bosville Macdonald family of Thorpe Hall, a lovely Georgian house a mile or so from the church. The monuments include a marble one with mourning angels supporting portrait medallions of Richard Beaumont (d. 1877) and his wife Susan (d. 1870), a daughter of Godfrey Bosville Macdonald, and another, also of marble, depicting a weeping woman holding a child.

The windows in the aisles contain nineteenth-century stained glass by Hodgson of York. All but one of the chancel windows, including the east window, and those in the east end of the aisles, contain stained glass designed by Hardman and inserted after the Second World War to replace nineteenth-century glass lost when the church was damaged by a bomb. The upper half of the one undamaged window, situated above the organ keyboard in the chancel, is by Arthur Ward and was inserted in 1915.

The lower half of this window depicts Sir Alexander Bosville Macdonald of the Isles (d. 1933) at the organ, surrounded by a choir of seventeen boys and men, their faces drawn from life. For some forty-six years Sir Alexander was organist and choirmaster of the church. A modern window in the south aisle was installed in his memory in 1955, and the church organ, built in 1888 by Messrs. Wordsworth & Co. of Leeds, was remodelled in 1933 as a further memorial to his services. The organ, whose keyboard is in the chancel, fills the west wall of the nave, covering the Norman tower arch and reaching to the roof.

Sir Alexander is buried in the elaborate family grave at the western edge of the churchyard, and close by is the somewhat simpler grave of the celebrated Yorkshire writer Winifred Holtby, who was born at Rudston in 1898 and died in 1935. An open book in white marble on her grave reads:

> God give me work till my life shall end
> And life till my work is done.

A memorial tablet inside the church, on the wall by the font, was erected by the Winifred Holtby Society, and reflects that 'Her work was notable for understanding, insight, and sincerity. Her charm as a woman came from gentle grace of manner, high courage and purpose, practical sympathy for others, and an endearing selflessness'.

Winifred Holtby was born at Rudston House, a large, detached farmhouse at the western edge of the village. She was the daughter of a prosperous farmer, who owned a number of farms in the area. In the social hierarchy of the day, which was still quite feudal, the Holtby family was second only to the Bosvilles of Thorpe Hall. Winifred's parents, David and Alice Holtby, took their social responsibilities seriously, and from them she inherited a concern for the oppressed, championing – among other causes – the African negro, Jews, and women. With her friend, Vera Brittain, Winifred Holtby is still renowned for her spirit of reforming zeal.

In Yorkshire, however, she is best remembered for her novels depicting life in the East Riding, in particular for 'South Riding'. For Winifred Holtby, the Wolds epitomised the beauty of the English countryside, and her books contain many evocative descriptions of the scenes she recalled from her childhood. Rudston itself features most prominently in her first novel, 'Anderby Wold', in which it appears as the village of Anderby. Thorpe Hall, the family home of the Bosvilles and Macdonalds, becomes Edenthorpe Hall, the home of the Setons.

Another of Rudston's claims to fame is the Roman villa, discovered to the south of the Rudston to Kilham road by a local farmer in 1933. Three fine mosaic pavements from the villa are now in the archaeology section of the Hull Transport Museum (housed in the former Corn Exchange). The largest of these pavements, known as the Venus pavement, depicts Venus with her hair streaming in the wind, an apple in one hand and a mirror in the other.

In addition to the mosaics, other Roman treasures were discovered during recent excavations, all of them now on display in the Hull Museum. These include floor tiles with the imprint of a man's nailed boot, and in 1971 the bones of two children were found, together with the skeleton of a man with a dagger in his back.

23

Thwing
All Saints

Continuing from Rudston in the direction of Sledmere along the B1253, you will soon see signposts for Thwing, which lies some eight miles north-west of Bridlington, a mile or so to the north of the B1253 road. The village is quietly situated in a green hollow, with a reed pond at its eastern end and the church high on a bank at the other end.

Thwing, now a tiny hamlet, was once a place of importance. The unusual name is Scandinavian in origin, and was formerly Tuuence, and more recently Tweng. Mentioned in Domesday, it was the seat of the de Thwing baronial family, who were kinsmen of the Yorkshire Bruces who sat on the throne of Scotland. John de Thwing, born c. 1320, became the greatest of all the priors of Bridlington. Known as St. John of Bridlington, he was the last Englishman to be canonised (in 1401) prior to the Reformation, and was born and educated in Thwing. As a child he attended the church daily for prayer. Robert de Thwing and Thomas de Thwing, of the same family, were in turn rectors of Thwing during John's lifetime.

In the time of Thomas à Becket, to whom a chapel in the church is dedicated, the village was granted a market charter but, though a network of roads still meets here, Thwing long ago ceased to be a major trading centre. It is now a peaceful, straggling country village with beautiful views across the Wolds landscape.

All Saints is a twelfth-century Norman church, and the chancel arch, south doorway and font, with its lozenge-shaped pattern, are all original Norman. The church was carefully restored by Temple Moore in 1900, and photographs of the building immediately before the restoration may be seen on the south wall by the font. The modern (south) porch of the church, in whose walls are inserted fragments of floriated crosses and window tracery, was erected in 1900 as a memorial to Thomas Lamplugh, who was born in 1615 at Octon, a mile away from Thwing, and who became Archbishop of York in 1688 (until 1691), assisting in the Coronation of William III. Before becoming Archbishop of York, he was principal of St. Alban's Hall, Oxford in 1664, Archdeacon of London from 1664–76, Vicar of St. Martin in the Fields in 1670, Dean of Rochester in 1672, and Bishop of Exeter in 1676.

Near the altar, on the south chancel wall, is a plaque with a tribute to Thomas Lamplugh. He presented to Thwing the Communion plate which is still used on major festivals, and which is engraved as follows: 'Thwing, in usum sacrae mensae D.D. Thomas Ebor 1689'. The south chancel window is also dedicated to Thomas Lamplugh D.D. Archbishop of York, and decorated with a mitre and shields and the royal insignia. His name is also preserved in Lamplugh House, for twelve years the home of a conference ministry run by the Rev. Lawrence Hoyle and his wife Margaret. In 1981 Mr. Hoyle helped establish Anglican Renewal ministries under the umbrella of the Lamplugh House Trust. This is an information and resource centre serving charismatic renewal in the Anglican church. By 1984 its work had expanded to such a degree that Mr. Hoyle felt obliged to move to other premises where the separate growth of ARM could be better accommodated. Lamplugh House, now under new wardenship, is still thriving as a renewal conference centre.

The church's Norman south doorway has shafts with spiral carving, elaborate capitals embellished with stars and chevron round the arch. A rare feature of the church is the well-preserved tympanum containing a sculpture of the Agnus Dei in a frame of zigzag. Inside the door, to the right, are the remains of a stoup.

The chancel arch, also Norman, is supported by three piers on either side, two with scalloped capitals, and the third richly carved with stars. The massive Norman tub font is decorated with a diaper pattern, and has cable mouldings on its top rim.

25

The narrow north aisle was added in the thirteenth-century, and is separated from the nave by an arcade of five piers. The east bay of the north aisle forms the Thomas à Becket chapel. On the east wall, above the altar of the chapel, is an unusual small panel with a worn stone carving of two figures. One of the figures – kneeling and (now) headless – is generally thought to be a monk at prayer, possibly Thomas à Becket himself.

To the right of the panel is a squint of unusual length giving a clear view from the chapel to the high altar. The abnormal length of the squint necessitated building an extra bulge on the external wall, at the corner between the chancel and the north aisle, in order to accommodate it. Under the squint is a projecting piscina with a trefoiled head.

Against the north aisle wall is a recumbent stone figure of a priest with a shaven head wearing a chasuble. A lion is at his feet, and angels at his head; his hands are at prayer, with a chalice beneath them. This is variously thought to be an effigy of John de Cotom, rector of Thwing from 1379 to 1426, who was buried in the chancel, or Robert de Thwing, who was rector in 1339.

Also on the north aisle wall are various tombstones with some rather charming verses:

> Farewell dear friends I must not stay,
> The great I am calls me away,
> Serve this great God for that you may,
> Triumphant rise, at the last day.

> Cease to lament that I am call'd away,
> And forc'd to leave my tenement of clay;
> The art of physic was in vain to save,
> My wasting body from the silent grave;
> Released from mortal cares with Heaven in view,
> I bid a vain and wicked world adieu,
> Raise then your hopes, to brighter realms above,
> Where we shall meet before the God of love;
> No mortal can resist the Lord's decree,
> Prepare to meet your God and follow me.

Much of the church was heavily restored and partly rebuilt in the late nineteenth early twentieth-century, when the low, embattled tower was rebuilt, and new windows were installed in the old walls of the chancel and the north aisle. John of Bridlington is commemorated in a modern stained-glass window in the north wall, along with St. Cecilia.

The church has some beautiful brass, including the lectern, and there is a lovely, carved oak pulpit with brass candelabra to the memory of William Arlton R.D., rector from 1883 to 1907, and also a prayer-desk.

Langtoft
St. Peter

Langtoft lies a few miles south of the B1253, along the B1249 Scarborough to Driffield road, and is situated in a deep hollow. The village suffered badly from a severe flood in the seventeenth century and another in 1892 during a terrific thunderstorm one Sunday when a local waterspout burst. Close to the village, the sides of the chalk Wolds still bear the scars of the water channels created as the water rushed down, carrying away trees and gates and hedges, flooding Langtoft to a depth of seven feet. The floods are commemorated on a plaque on one of the houses in the centre of the village.

The church, not immediately visible from the main road through the village, is on a steep hillside just north of a road leading to Sledmere. It was restored for Sir Tatton Sykes by Charles Hodgson Fowler early this century. Sir Tatton also gave the village a beautiful cross on three steps, its base carved with

27

eight panels depicting scenes of country life, its shaft carved with a canopied saint. This stands close to the smaller of the village's two ponds.

The tower of the church and parts of the nave are from the thirteenth-century, but, though the south arcade still retains some of its thirteenth-century pillars, the nave as a whole was restored c. 1926, resulting in a strange variety of pillars. The fourteenth-century (Decorated) chancel has a trefoiled piscina and three fine sedilia with richly carved canopies. The chancel arch is Perpendicular.

A variety of saints and celebrities, most of them fairly 'local', occupy the stained glass of the windows in the south aisle: Wilfrid, who built and founded the monastery of Ripon where he was buried in AD 709; Chad, Bishop of Northumbria, who founded Lichfield Cathedral; Aidan, Bishop of Lindisfarne, who came from Iona at the request of King Oswald to instruct the English in Christianity in AD 651; Oswald of Northumbria himself, who was slain in battle in AD 642 by Pewda, the Pagan king of Mercia; John of Beverley; Hilda of Whitby; King Edwin and Queen Ethelburga of Northumbria, with Paulinus between them; and Edward the Confessor in a small, trefoiled lancet to the east of the south aisle.

The church's modern font has eight saints carved in niches, and eight more round its oak cover, which has a traceried spire. The gem of the church, however, is a twelfth-century Norman font recovered from Cottam, along with a number of headstones. Cottam is one of the many deserted villages in this part of Yorkshire. Like several other Wolds villages, it was depopulated in the fifteenth and sixteenth-centuries, and then saw a substantial increase in its population in early Victorian times. A survey of 1841 revealed that, although there were only two inhabited farmsteads at Cottam, they housed forty-one people, as all the farm employees lived on the premises. Coincidentally, a similar situation appertained at Cowlam, two miles away, the site of another deserted mediaeval village, where forty-four inhabitants occupied two farmsteads in the mid nineteenth century.

Both the church at Cottam and that at Cowlam were rebuilt last century, and both had large Norman fonts – the one from Cottam being now at Langtoft (see photograph). The figure carvings on the two fonts are so similar that it is more than likely that both are by the same hand, with the rather less elaborate Cowlam font pre-dating the Cottam one by a few years. The two fonts date from the early to mid twelfth-century and, while resembling each other closely, differ from other Norman fonts in the area.

The central scene on both fonts depicts Adam and Eve at either side of the Tree of Knowledge. The only features which distinguish Eve from Adam are her long hair and wide hips. Entwined round the tree is the serpent, bearing the forbidden fruit in its rather dragon-like mouth. Eve's right hand is extended to receive the fruit, while Adam is already holding a piece of fruit. This telescoping of events was a common mediaeval device. Adam and Eve are also holding large leaves to conceal their nakedness.

At one side of this scene, the Cottam font has a carving of another tree, with lush, interlacing branches, probably representing the Tree of Life as a counter to the evil influence of the Tree of Knowledge, and at the other is the martyrdom of St. Andrew, with two men fastening him to his cross. Then comes a carving of a dragon, often used to represent Satan, followed by the martydom of St. Lawrence, who is being attacked by a man with a spear. St. Margaret of Antioch is shown being swallowed by a large dragon, with her feet and skirt protruding from its mouth, while her head emerges from its back.

Against the west wall by the font at Langtoft are stones with Norman carving, and the remains of the mediaeval nave of the church can still be seen in the Old Vicarage garden.

Sledmere
St. Mary

A minor road from Langtoft joins the B1253 to the village of Sledmere, famous for the Sykes family who have over the years done so much to improve the Yorkshire Wolds by planting trees and hedgerows and also by restoring numerous Wold churches.

St. Mary's church stands within the grounds of Sledmere House, though fenced off from access to the house itself. The entrance is directly opposite the war memorial designed by the late Col. Mark Sykes in tribute to the Wold Wagoners, who were among the first civilians to fight in World War I. About 1200 men from farms in the Yorkshire Wolds volunteered for Sir Mark's 'Wagoners' Reserve' in 1912, ready to be called up, if needed, for transport work involving horses. They were paid a retaining fee of £1 a year, and soon after the Great War started they found themselves in France.

The monument's panels of low-relief carvings depict the 'Wagoners' engaged in driving competitions, at work, joining up, bidding farewell to their loved ones, on the sea, disembarking, and putting the Germans to flight. An integral part of the war memorial is a sixty-feet high 'Eleanor Cross', erected by Sir Tatton in 1900, to which brass plaques were added in 1919. The Eleanor Cross is a copy by Temple Moore of the one at Northampton, and is so called in memory of Queen Eleanor, the wife of Edward I. When she died in the north and was taken down to London for burial, King Edward had a cross of this type erected at every spot where her body rested.

The church of St. Mary is generally considered to be one of the loveliest modern parish churches in Yorkshire. It was rebuilt for Sir Tatton Sykes by Temple Moore in 1898, in the style of the fourteenth-century, and is one of the best and most lavish of his restorations, with a fine array of sculpture, woodwork, and stained glass.

The porch has an elaborate vaulted roof of red and white stone, its bosses carved with, inter alia, the signs of the Four Evangelists, an Agnus Dei, and a Madonna. The door into the church has tiny panels of tracery and is set within a richly moulded doorway of pinkish stone.

The walls inside the church also have a pinkish glow, which is intensified by the proliferation of stained glass. The north and south aisles have vaulted roofs like the porch, while the nave and chancel are wagon-roofed. The south aisle has a trefoiled piscina and a tiny doorway in the corner to its right. Around the top of the piscina are minute stone carvings representing the Passion story. First is a carving of a small money bag, then a lantern, an ear and sword, a scourge, a cock, a cross with hammer and nails, a coat with three dice, a sponge on a stick, and finally three jars containing the spices for preparing the body for burial.

Under canopies on the east wall of the north aisle are carvings of the Madonna and child with two saints at either side. The east walls of both aisles are carved with an intricate floral design, and both aisles have altars.

In the place of a chancel arch is an elaborate oak screen, and the chancel itself is extremely ornate. The windows on each side are framed by traceried arches on columns; under them runs a stringcourse of flowers, and between the windows are statues of saints under richly carved canopies.

The colourful east window, known as a 'Jesse' window, reaches to the roof. At the bottom of the centre panel is the sleeping figure of Jesse. Above him is David, then Solomon, then the infant Jesus. The two panels on either side show the twelve kings of Israel, all named, and the two outer panels depict twelve prophets. The top portion of the window shows people rising from the dead, then comes the figure of Justice, representing the final Judgement, and at the very top is the figure of Christ in Glory. The reredos features the Crucifixion, along with finely carved figures of the Apostles.

Amongst the fine carvings to the right of the altar is what is probably the first memorial to Queen Victoria, who died at the time when the carvings were being done. The one commemorating her shows a crown, a V, and the word 'obiit'. Various members of the Sykes family are also commemorated in the church, and the bust of Sir Tatton (d. 1913), which each of the churches restored by him is meant to display, is clearly in evidence at the back of the north aisle.

A spiral staircase from a door in the south wall to the left of the entrance to the church leads to a small study furnished with the favourite books of the late Colonel Mark Sykes. (This is normally kept locked).

In a glass case in the north aisle is the hand-made 'Book of Remembrance' of the 1914–18 war. The names and deeds of the soldiers from the various Wolds villages are recorded in the form of a mediaeval psalter within the book's wooden covers. Beeford, near Skipsea, is represented in pictorial form by bees in flight, a hive, and a woman crossing a ford; Skipsea itself is depicted by a girl skipping beside the sea, accompanied by some jumping fish; for Rudston a winged devil drops the famous monolith beside the church; Weaverthorpe has a man busy at his handloom; and Sledmere is represented by people sledging on the frozen mere (now drained) in front of Sledmere House. In the final picture, Sir Mark and a friend are depicted in the chamber above the south porch.

One of the most spectacular of the Sykes' monuments is on Garton Hill, midway between Sledmere and Garton-on-the-Wolds. A slender, four-sided tower of grey and brown stone stands 120 feet high, 450 feet above sea-level, and is a landmark for miles around. It was erected by the tenants of the Sykes' estates in 1865 in memory of Sir Tatton (d. 1863). At the base of the tower are panels carved in relief, depicting a pastoral scene and Sir Tatton on horseback, his tall hat in his hand. The tower tapers towards the top, and is surmounted by an elaborate cross. 4th baronet, known as 'Old Tat' or 'Old Tatters', became a legendary figure throughout Yorkshire, and tales of his remarkable feats of stamina and determination still abound today. He is reported to have ridden from Yorkshire to Aberdeen to act as a jockey for Lord Huntley in a race, which he duly won, and then back to Doncaster in time for the St. Leger, which he never missed – a journey of 740 miles in five days. One morning he allegedly rode the sixty-three miles from Sledmere to Pontefract to take part in a race during the afternoon, then went on to Doncaster, where he stayed the night, continuing to Lincoln the next day for a four-mile race in the afternoon. He was also renowned as a good squire who looked well after all his employees.

Sir Tatton also began the work of restoring Wolds churches, employing Pearson to restore Kirkburn and Garton-on-the-Wolds. The work was continued indefatigably by his son, also Sir Tatton (d. 1913), who built or restored more than twenty churches throughout the East Riding, twelve of them on the Sledmere estates. He was the patron of many of the most famous Gothic revival architects of the Victorian era, employing first George Edmund Street, then Hodgson Fowler and Temple Moore.

Kirby Grindalythe
St. Andrew

Kirby Grindalythe lies to the north of Sledmere and can be reached via a minor road leading from opposite the gates of Sledmere church. As the road approaches Kirby Grindalythe, there is a clear view of the church and its magnificent spire across the fields.

Another of the several villages along the Gypsey Race which runs down the Wold valley, Kirby Grindalythe consists of only a handful of houses and cottages and a couple of farms, but its church attracts coach-loads of visitors to the village each year.

The origins of the village's unusual name suggest that there was a church on the site in the late tenth or early eleventh century, for it is referred to in the Domesday Survey of 1086 as 'Chirchebi', i.e. 'the church village'. The distinctive 'Grindalythe' part of the name derives from 'in Crendalith', meaning 'on the side of the crane-valley', and was added at some time before 1367. Further evidence for a pre-Conquest church is to be found in the fragments of an Anglo-Danish cross, now built into the interior walls of the tower.

In the early part of the twelfth-century, Walter l'Espec gave the church to Kirkham Priory along with Garton-on-the-Wolds, as part of its original endowments, and it appears to have been rebuilt in the Norman period. A north aisle was added in the late twelfth or early thirteenth-century, as well as a vesica and two lancet windows in the east wall of the chancel. Kirby Grindalythe's first vicar was appointed in 1305.

The church was restored, indeed practically rebuilt, for the second Sir Tatton Sykes by George Edmund Street, who began his restoration work in 1872.

St. Andrew's church lies at the end of a lane to the west of the village, across the Gypsey Race which runs alongside the lane. It is approached through an elaborate stone lychgate with a vaulted, pyramid-shaped roof, battlements, lancets and gargoyles. In the churchyard is a gabled cross, designed by Temple Moore, which is carved with a crucifixion scene and the signs of the Four Evangelists. Near the cross are some stone seats.

Of the Norman church only the lower part of the tower retains its original form, although Street did re-use some Norman masonry in the chancel, and the remains of the old Norman font have been built into the interior south-east wall of the tower. The belfry dates from the fourteenth-century, as do two of the four bells (the others were cast in 1667 and 1876). The octagonal mediaeval spire, which makes the church such a landmark, was largely rebuilt in 1718, and is again badly in need of repair, as is the tower, the sum of £21,000 being required to meet the cost of the work.

The nave and chancel were completely rebuilt in 1872, the

nave in mid thirteenth-century style, and the chancel in Norman style. The north aisle had disappeared by this time, and the nave and chancel were divided by a wall with a door in the centre. Street restored the north arcade and the north aisle, using old foundations, and added the north chapel with a vestry to the east. The stone tomb under the round-arched recess in the north chapel is frequently alleged to be that of the founder of the church. The bold arcading on the side of the tomb is very similar to that on some Norman fonts.

The famous mosaic on the west wall of the nave is the main attraction for the surprisingly large numbers of tourists who visit the church each week during the summer months. It is of – as yet unidentified – Italian workmanship and was executed a few years after the main restoration of the church by Street (not, as has apparently been suggested, by Italian prisoners-of-war during World War II!). The mosaic, which extends right to the roof, depicts Christ being received into glory, surrounded by angels and watched from below by Mary and the eleven faithful apostles. An open book carries the Latin text: 'Ego sum resurrectio et vita'.

Although the roof of Kirby Grindalythe church is – unusually for a Street restoration – without colour (supposedly due to a sudden fit of economy by Sir Tatton), there is plenty of colour elsewhere in the building. This is not only evident in the vast mosaic, but also in the lavish use of coloured glazed tiles in the chancel floor, and the attractive stained glass, most of which is by Clayton and Bell (who completed their work in 1878). The three large windows on the south side of the nave, however, are by Burlison and Grylls. They illustrate, from east to west, St. Andrew, the church's patron saint, with St. Paul; St. William of York and St. Augustine (of Canterbury); St. Stephen, the first Christian martyr, and St. Alban, the first British martyr.

The east window in the chancel, depicts the Annunciation, with the angel on one side of the altar and Mary on the other. Above, in an oval window, is the Holy Spirit shown as a dove. The stained glass in the south wall of the chancel represents, from east to west, St. Ann teaching the Virgin Mary to read; the Virgin Mary herself; St. Joachim; and, in a low window behind the choir stalls, Mary and Jesus in the stable; then comes the presentation of Jesus in the Temple, with Simeon.

The reredos of white marble and alabaster, by James Redfern, has the Crucifixion in the centre, with a sculpture of St. Andrew on his X-shaped cross at one side, and St. Peter on his inverted cross at the other. Pearson may have been responsible for the final form of the reredos, which was not completed until 1879, although Redfern died in 1876.

There are two restored sedilia and a piscina in the chancel, and the remains of various floriated crosses are built into the exterior wall of the chancel on the south side and at the east end.

The plain oak chancel-screen, by Rattee and Kett, is surmounted by a carved crucifix and figures of St. Mary and St. John. Carved in the wall above the screen is a vesica with a seated figure of Christ in majesty – a miniature version of the one at North Newbald.

The marble pulpit, with its attractive inlay in red, white, gold and green, was probably designed by Street, as was the brass lectern in the form of an eagle, which was copied from one found in a lake at Newstead Abbey.

33

Wharram-Le-Street
St. Mary

From Kirby Grindalythe the B1248 leads south-east to the village of Wharram-le-Street, which, as the latter part of its name suggests, stands on the site of a Roman road which ran from Malton to the Humber. This small, peaceful village stands high on the Wolds, some six miles south-east of Malton. From the churchyard there are views across the Vale of Pickering to the Moors. The Gypsey Race rises nearby in what was the courtyard of a Romano-British villa.

The church is hidden away at one side of the village, close to the cross-roads. It is a simple, unspoilt building of Saxon origin, subsequently extended and embellished by the Normans. The original design of the church (a square-ended chancel, an oblong nave, and a square west tower) has been preserved, despite the various additions and alterations over the centuries. There is evidence of Saxon work in the tower, which is the oldest of any Wold church, and the Rev. William Everitt, former vicar of Wharram-le-Street, inclines to the view that it is older than the date of c. 1050 which has been given for its construction. He believes that a late Saxon top may have been added to a much earlier structure. The total height of the tower is now fifty-one feet, and it is built of courses of roughly squared stones.

The four belfry windows are late Saxon in style, each window consisting of two narrow openings divided by a plain cylindrical shaft. Long vertical stones flank the sides of the windows, and a long horizontal slab, carried through to the inside of the tower, rests on the top of the deeply recessed shafts – a typical feature of Saxon architecture.

The original and striking west doorway (see photograph), tall, narrow, and embellished with Norman columns, is now blocked and transformed into a window crowned with a

35

horseshoe-shaped arch. The horseshoe shape, which was a fashion in Norman arches not very common in this country, is also featured in the high tower arch, which is a larger version of the west doorway arch.

The south doorway, within a tiny porch, may be Saxon in origin, but is decorated with carving of a more advanced type than that of the west doorway or tower arch. The arch is of two orders, an inner square order, and an outer order which resembles that of the west doorway. It has a shallow hood-moulding consisting of an outer face decorated with chevron and an inner roll-moulding and is probably of a later date than the west doorway and tower arch.

The Saxon nave was altered by the Normans, and the north aisle was added in the fourteenth-century. The east and west walls of the nave are original, as is the eastern part of the north wall between the nave and the aisle. With the addition of the north aisle, the north wall was cut through to form an arcade of two unequal arches which are thought to have been built at slightly different times. A double respond divides the two arches. The south wall was completely rebuilt in the nineteenth-century – apparently on the original foundation. A small pointed chancel arch of two orders has been built onto the original Norman columns, and the chancel itself was rebuilt in 1862. Only the three-light east window has stained glass: this represents the Good Shepherd flanked by two angels.

There are strong resemblances between this church and one many miles away from Yorkshire, but close to my present abode, namely the St. Regulus chapel at St. Andrews, Fife. At the time of the Domesday Survey the manor of Wharram was held under Robert of Mortain by Nigel Fossard. The latter's son, Robert, gave Wharram to Nostell Priory, and it was from there that King Alexander of Scotland brought monks to St. Andrews by way of Scone and it was one of those monks who became Bishop Robert of St. Andrews.

The most striking similarity between Wharram church and St. Regulus' chapel at St. Andrews is in the design of the arches in the two churches. Not only do the arches have similar mouldings, they also share the unusual feature of having the two orders of the arch set side by side instead of one over the other. Taylor and Taylor (Anglo-Saxon Architecture Volume II) are of the opinion that the arches in each case were an addition, by masons from Nostell, to an earlier structure, rather than the two churches being built by the same master mason.

The plain drum font (inside the tower vestry) is early Norman. Inside the ringing chamber can be seen a blocked internal doorway which formerly opened onto the nave. The round-headed doorway is two feet wide and six feet four inches in height. There are two bells in the belfry, one mediaeval, one seventeenth-century, which were brought from Wharram Percy when the church there was closed.

Wharram Percy
St. Martin

A couple of miles or so south-west of Wharram-le-Street, just off the B1248, a lane leads to Burdale, once famous for the now disused Burdale Tunnel, and D of E signs point the way to the deserted village of Wharram Percy. As a visit to Wharram Percy involves a walk of over a mile, it is advisable to choose a fine day for viewing this particular church, which stands in a lonely valley along with some attractive farm cottages. Excavations have been going on here for the past thirty-five years, and are still continuing.

There are over a hundred deserted villages in the East Riding, and Wharram Percy is one of the most famous of them, and the only one in the care of the Department of the Environment. The area was first settled in pre-historic times.

37

Roman remains have been discovered around and under the church as well as a Roman fort on top of the hill to the north of the village. The twenty-acre village was abandoned over 500 years ago (c. 1500). It was first affected by the Black Death c. 1350, but it was the rise of the cloth-making industry in Yorkshire which really depopulated the village, by making it more profitable for landowners to concentrate on sheep-rearing rather than growing corn, thus making large numbers of ploughmen redundant.

When I wrote to the clergy of all the churches I intended visiting to check that they would be open to visitors, the Rev. William Everitt wrote back to me about the churches of Wharram-le-Street and Wharram Percy assuring me that: 'Both churches are open, Wharram Percy particularly so as there is no roof on it and it is a ruin'! The church was in use until 1949, but the lead was stolen from the roof and the building rapidly then fell into ruin.

The earliest church at Wharram Percy was of timber, then came a stone church which had a small chancel added at a later date. It was rebuilt in the late eleventh-century, and of this building the west wall and arch still survive. The chancel was constructed on a raft of chalk blocks extending the natural terrace into the valley. In the early twelfth-century a tower was added at the west end of the nave: it has a plain, early Norman arch. The south aisle was added in the late twelfth-century and the north aisle in the early thirteenth. In the late thirteenth-century a new, square-ended chancel was built on an extended chalk raft. When the congregation declined c. 1500, both aisles were demolished, and the blocked arches can be seen in the north and south walls.

The fourteenth-century windows now in the north wall of the nave came from the demolished north aisle. A blocked doorway in the south-east corner of the nave re-uses late Saxon capitals and a pointed arch composed of twelfth-century stone with zigzag carving. The old chancel became unsafe in the seventeenth-century and was replaced by the present, smaller one.

The church served five townships within its parish: Wharram itself, Burdale, Raisthorpe, Towthorpe, and Thixendale. Until 1870, when a new church was built at Thixendale, the parishioners had to walk the three miles to Wharram Percy to attend church. (The other three villages are now only isolated farmsteads).

The Norman font from Wharram Percy, decorated with nailhead ornament and wide arcading, is now at St. Michael's church, Orchard Park Road, Hull. It was moved there when Wharram Percy church began to deteriorate rapidly.

The mediaeval vicarage was approximately twenty-five yards to the north of the church, but in the sixteenth-century it was moved further north, and the foundations of a huge Georgian vicarage have also been discovered. In 1834 the parish was combined with that of Wharram-le-Street, and the vicarage was given up.

The early settlement at Wharram Percy was on the hill immediately to the west of the church. Nearby, in the late twelfth-century, the famous Percy family, remembered in the name of the village, built their manor house, subsequently abandoning it in favour of a site further up the hill to the north. The size of the church indicates its former importance, and it is still an impressive structure, even in its present ruined state – well worth the walk!

Fimber
St. Mary

If you rejoin the B1248 after leaving Wharram Percy and head south, you will soon reach the B1251 road from Sledmere to Fridaythorpe. Fimber is a tiny place on a hill along this road in the direction of Fridaythorpe. The church here was built by Street for Sir Tatton Sykes and was consecrated on 13th April 1871 by the Archbishop of York.

The churchyard is entered by an attractive stone lychgate, designed by Street, which has a little cross gable over the apex of the arch. A small avenue of yews leads up to the church. St. Mary's is erected on a Bronze-Age barrow that once served as an Anglian burial ground.

A celebrated inhabitant of Fimber was John Mortimer, who was born in 1825 and who devoted many years to excavating old graves. He wrote a classic book on British and Saxon burial mounds, and assembled a notable collection of flints and pottery.

According to John Hutchinson in his booklet 'George Edmund Street in East Yorkshire', the original design of the church differs rather drastically from its execution. Instead of the simplicity of the original conception, there is what John Hutchinson describes as 'a proliferation of extra buttresses... gabletted and cross-gabletted and offset in a variety of ways: the tower has acquired clasping buttresses and some ragged polychromy in the arcaded belfry. The building has lost its simplicity of statement, and not gained much in the process'. He suggests that perhaps Sir Tatton wished to compensate for the size of this, his smallest church, by a more elaborate design than that initially envisaged.

Whatever the reason for the change in plan, John Hutchinson's criticisms are perhaps rather harsh, particularly his subsequent comment that the interior of the church has a 'faded feeling' which not even the Clayton and Bell glass is able to brighten. Far from seeming either unduly cluttered with buttresses externally or having a 'faded' interior, I thought Fimber church one of the most attractive I have visited recently. As with the tiny church at Scorborough, near Beverley, its admittedly rather elaborate ornamentation did not strike me as being obtrusive, but gives the building a certain charm, which is considerably enhanced by its pleasant location.

Inside, the church has a neat and well-kept appearance, and several interesting features. The chancel has a coloured tile floor and a roof decorated with gold stars. There are two trefoiled, arched sedilia in the south chancel wall – although John Hutchinson rightly comments that any priest who sat in them 'would have to have his knees on either side of the altar rail!' The stained glass of the east window depicts the Crucifixion, Resurrection and Ascension.

St. Mary's has a particularly fine brass chancel screen on a stone base decorated with quatrefoils. The corona on the screen fell off in March 1874 while it was being cleaned, and has now been taken elsewhere. Other noteworthy features include the tiny stone pulpit, and the octagonal font, decorated on four sides with quatrefoil, and an ornate marble reredos.

40

Fridaythorpe
St. Mary

Fridaythorpe lies eleven miles west of Driffield on a sharp bend of the A166, the Bridlington to York road. The village stands more than 500 feet above sea-level, and, while its proximity to the busy A166 precludes it from enjoying the tranquillity of many of the villages on the Wolds, Fridaythorpe is not without its attractions, notably a green with two large ponds.

The quaint church is extremely difficult to find. It lies down a long lane to the north of the main road, from which it is hidden by a farm and some beech trees. There is a lovely view from the churchyard to the north across the fields of the Wolds.

A solid, simple building, St. Mary's is a small Norman church of the twelfth century, restored in 1902 by Charles Hodgson Fowler for Sir Tatton Sykes. It has a curious, squat tower with sturdy walls and an attractive black and white clock on the west wall. This clock, which is dated 1903, has a wooden face copied from a clock in an eighteenth-century French chateau and bears the apt inscription: 'Time is short, Eternity long'. Inside the tower the works of the clock can be seen.

Within the south porch is a splendid Norman doorway, its arch richly decorated with three orders of zigzag and its capitals all differently carved. Inside, the plain, circular font is also Norman, as is the chancel arch, which is decorated with one order of zigzag.

Above the pulpit is a small square window, known as a rood window, the light from which falls naturally on the keystone of the chancel arch. This stone has on it a small carving of the Risen Christ, with the empty tomb shown in the bottom left-hand corner.

On the floor of the chancel is the coffin lid of a priest depicting a chalice and Bible, which dates from c. 1350, and several coffin lids from the churchyard have been used in restoring the church, notably in the lintels of the three clerestory windows and just below the pinnacles of the tower.

In the north wall of the chancel is a blocked Norman window. The south wall contains a round-headed priest's doorway, two thirteenth-century lancet windows, a piscina and aumbry, and a sedilia formed by lowering the sill of one of the lancets. The beautifully carved oak altar table came from Sledmere church and depicts the Madonna on the front panel. The reredos features Christ flanked by angels in the centre, with two Evangelists in each of the side panels. The altar rails are Jacobean, dating from c. 1620.

During Sir Tatton's restoration of the church, the north aisle was re-built and the original thirteenth-century arcade which had been blocked up was opened up again. On the east column of the arcade is the rather perplexing inscription: 'This 713 found hear'. What exactly was found (if anything) remains a mystery.

A fragment of an old cross is built into the exterior west wall of the aisle, and just above it is a stone with a carving of a peacock. Like the figure on the chancel arch, the bird is very crudely carved, and its identification as a peacock is purely by virtue of its long tail and clumsy feet. The peacock was a part of the animal symbolism in the bestiary, so popular in the early Middle Ages. The flesh of the peacock was said to be incorruptible and thus came to represent the resurrection of the dead. Many a moral was also drawn from the contrast between the bird's surface beauty and the ugliness of its feet and its awkward gait. On the south outside wall, just below the nave window, is a scratch dial.

An unusual feature of the church is the screenwork separating the aisle from the nave and the pews from the west end. The oak screens and pews were added during Sir Tatton's restoration at the beginning of the century. On the screen to the right of the entrance are some old photographs of the church as it was in 1894, before its restoration. Beside the photographs is a list of the church's vicars, the first recorded one being John de Brown in 1320.

42

43

Bishop Wilton
St. Edith

From Fridaythorpe head in the York direction along the A166 for a few miles until you reach the lane to Bishop Wilton. The village lies a mile to the south of the A166, at the foot of Garrowby Hill. The back lane to it passes the site of a summer palace of the Archbishops of York – hence the name Bishop Wilton.

The settlement of the village of Wilton dates back to Saxon times. The manor was given by King Athelstan (915–940) to the Archbishop of York, Wulstannus. Archbishop Grey (1216–55) built the palace at the eastern end of the village and its name was extended at that time to its present form. The outline of the palace can still be seen in the field beyond the school.

Bishop Wilton is one of the most attractive villages in the East Riding. A stream flows through a deep, grassy hollow in the middle of the village and is crossed by footbridges. On the banks at each side of the stream are old cottages and brick houses. The church of St. Edith lies behind the houses on the north bank.

Norman in origin, the church was tastefully restored for Sir Tatton Sykes by J. L. Pearson in 1858–59 at a cost of between £3000 and £4000, and is considered by many to be one of the best pieces of restoration work which Pearson carried out for Sir Tatton. Street also had a hand in the restoration: he designed the chancel screen and also provided designs for other artistic work.

The remarkable flooring of a black and white marble mosaic by Salviati is copied from a floor in the Vatican which was itself originally in the palace of the Caesars at Rome. The design is composed of various different species of birds in a pattern of scrolls.

Some original Norman work is to be found in the chancel, which retains much of its old masonry and its original arch. The tall, wide arch has three orders on its west face, an outer one of beakhead and an inner order of zigzag.

The Norman arch of the south doorway is of four orders, with an unusual and quite elaborately carved inner order of small arches cutting across roll mouldings. On the stones of the outer order are carvings of a seated man warming his hands at a fire; a bishop in elaborate vestments (possibly related to the village's connection with the Archbishops of York); some soldiers; a figure carrying a severed head; and a variety of animal carvings. Many of these animal carvings date from the church's restoration in the late nineteenth-century, but among the original Norman stones are a lion with a well-carved tail and striking eyes; a centaur (representing man's baser nature) shooting at his foe, depicted as a human face; an unusual carving of a baboon or monkey playing a drum or tambourine; and dragons consuming human beings. It is possible that the lion and centaur, both popular symbols from the bestiary, also had zodiacal significance (Leo and Sagittarius), and among the modern stones are a Pisces and a goat, which could represent Capricorn. However, it is not clear how faithful the modern carvings are to the original stones.

St. Edith's, dating from the fourth phase of Norman architecture (from 1150–60), is the most elaborate church of its period in the area. The widespread use of figure and animal carving on the south doorway – all of it of a high quality – is the first known use of carvings of this type in the region.

Stone carving of a rather more recent date adorns the modern font, which has figures of John the Baptist, St. Cuthbert, St. Chad, St. Paulinus, St. Philip, St. Wilfred, St. Oswald and St. Columba. The cover, in the form of a traceried tower and spire, features the four Evangelists alternating with the four doctors of the western church – St. Gregory, St. Augustine of Hippo, St. Jerome and St. Ambrose.

The eighty-feet long nave has thirteenth-century arcades with very short pillars. The two aisles were added in the mid fourteenth-century, and the tower and the 120 feet high spire were built slightly later. At the north of the nave, projecting from the north aisle, is a small transept with a reticulated north window. A piscina with a projecting bowl is cut into the east respond of the north arcade, and there is another piscina in the chancel.

The hammerbeam roof of the nave and chancel is beautifully decorated in gold and colour. Some 8000 gold leaves were used in the work. The reredos is a copy of a Flemish triptych of the Crucifixion, originally from Bruges and now in a museum in Cologne. It was a gift from Sir Tatton.

The stained glass windows in the chancel, by Clayton and Bell, depict scenes of the New Testament foreshadowed in the Old, and are made up of tiny pieces of glass to produce a jewel-like, late twelfth-century effect. This work may have been carried out under Pearson's direction. The west window is a memorial to Sir Tatton Sykes and his wife Mary Anne, erected by their daughter in 1864. St. Edith, the church's patron saint, is shown in the centre light, flanked by King Athelstan and St. John of Beverley.

Pocklington
All Saints

Pocklington, some five miles south of Bishop Wilton, is a popular market town at the foot of the steeply-sloping Wolds and is a point of intersection for several minor roads. For centuries Pocklington has been one of the few important market centres for Wold farmers – along with Beverley and Driffield. The railway and the Pocklington Canal helped trade to flourish, and at the end of the nineteenth-century Pocklington's main industries were corn-milling, brewing, iron founding, and the growing of flax. In addition to the town's regular markets, there were also four fairs a year.

The reformer William Wilberforce attended school in Pocklington between 1771–76. When his family settled in Yorkshire, they took their name from the nearby village of Wilberfoss. The grammar school he attended in Pocklington was founded in 1514 by Archdeacon John Dolman and was rebuilt last century.

The 120 feet high Perpendicular tower (c. 1420) of the mainly mediaeval parish church dominates the town. Foundations of an early Saxon church have been discovered under the present building, and odd fragments of a Norman church remain, but most of the existing church dates from the late twelfth to the early fifteenth-century.

The church is a large cruciform structure and has several notable features. The early thirteenth-century north arcade has grotesque carvings on the hoods of its pointed arches, and on the capitals are various curious figures, including a horizontal human form, two men crawling through bushes, two men wrestling, and a beast with a human head meeting a bird with an animal head. Legend has it that the two men wrestling are the master mason and his son, the carving having been carried out by the son in order to prove his ability when told by his father that he was too inexperienced to carve. Alternatively, it could represent Jacob wrestling with the angel.

The south arcade, the south doorway with its rich mouldings, and the outer, Early English doorway of the porch arch date from c. 1250. The porch itself was blown down in 1884, and the present one was dedicated on 6 May, 1885. The porch floor, of Minton tiles, was subscribed by children of the parish. Within the porch are fragments of Norman carving – zigzag mouldings, a beakhead, and the head of a cat. It has been suggested that the cat's head was part of a heathen image, a relic of the site's probably former use as a heathen shrine, dug up from under the porch where it had been placed so that Christian feet might walk over it.

The font bowl dates from the eleventh-century and is a single piece of fossil limestone. The original base disappeared some time ago, and in 1881 a red brick base which had replaced it was discarded for the present, more elaborate structure, whose marble pillars have pre-historic shells embedded in them.

The church's most notable possession is the beautifully sculptured Sotheby Cross, situated to the north of the font under one of the tower arches. The cross dates from the fourteenth-century and was discovered in 1835 buried in the churchyard, where it had probably been hidden for safety during the Civil War. John Sotheby is depicted on the west face of the cross, and a Latin inscription on the shaft asks us to pray for his soul. On the north face is a sculpture of God the Father holding a crucifix with a dove above Him (a representation of the Trinity); on the south face is the Crucifixion; and the east face shows Paulinus with crozier and vestments.

A Latin inscription on the (restored) base tells us that Paulinus preached and celebrated mass here in AD 627. The inscription is said to have been copied from an old stone which lay by the cross and which gives some indication of the date of the church's foundation. AD 627 was the year in which King Edwin of Northumbria was converted to Christianity by Paulinus after the Great Council and the subsequent destruction of the heathen temple at Goodmanham. It is probable that Paulinus and the rest of the company stopped off at Pocklington on the way to York and baptised some of the first converts to Christianity in the stream which runs on the north side of the church.

In the north wall of the chancel is a thirteenth-century doorway to the Lady Chapel and a thirteenth-century arch to the St. Nicholas aisle in the north transept. The chapel dates from c. 1320, and the chancel itself was rebuilt a century later. The clerestory of the nave was installed at the same time, and the west tower added.

The pulpit was designed by Temple Moore and carved by Messrs. Elwell of Beverley in 1881. Its panels depict the Good Samaritan, Peter and John healing the lame man, and angels with shields. The pulpit was provided by public subscription in memory of Dr. Thomas Wilson. A former curate of the church sought to 'improve' the carving by reducing the size of the noses of the figures!

Beneath the pulpit is a gravestone with a floriated cross and an inscription in Latin to Margaret Esyngwald (Easingwald), Prioress of a Benedictine nunnery at Wilberfoss in the early sixteenth-century. According to legend, she and John Dolman (or Dowman), who founded Pocklington School in 1514, were in love. He was in holy orders and therefore unable to marry, so she became a nun. When she died, her spirit haunted the nunnery, so the nuns supposedly moved her body to be near John Dolman, in order that she might find peace.

The slab which bears her name was moved to its present site from the St. Nicholas aisle, and near it was found a skeleton with a token in the left eye socket. Another broken stone slab was found five feet below the surface of the floor of the St. Nicholas aisle, and on it were carved the letters J. D.

In St. Nicholas's aisle is a fifteenth-century double stall for the headmaster of the grammar school, and a low screen with three fifteenth-century panels.

Against the south wall of the chancel is another of the church's treasures, the Denison Memorial. The carved wooden panels were made for a reredos and were brought back from Italy by a member of the Denison family, although the work is German, dating from c. 1500. The three large panels show Christ carrying his cross, the Crucifixion scene with Christ between the two thieves and Roman soldiers keeping back the crowd, and the dead Christ in the arms of his mother. In the smaller panels is an interesting collection of scenes, including a nun at prayer, a child kneeling at an altar, the holy family with the wise men, a castle, a canopied bed, and a woman riding a camel.

On the external east wall of the chancel is an inscription to the Flying Man, Thomas Pelling, who was killed in 1733 while sliding down a rope fixed at one end to a pinnacle of the church tower and at the other end to a windlass near an inn. He had makeshift wings attached to his arms and legs, and one heel was attached to a pulley running on the rope. His death was caused by the rope becoming slack and flinging him against the battlements. He was buried where he fell.

GLOSSARY

Anglo-Saxon	Used to denote the period before the Norman Conquest in 1066.
Arcade	A series of arches supported on pillars.
Aumbry	A recess or cupboard to hold the sacred vessels used in Holy Communion.
Bestiary	A book very popular in the Middle Ages, consisting of a collection of moralized fables, mostly about animals.
Boss	A knob-like projecting ornament at intersecting points, usually the beams of a roof.
Box pew	A pew with a high wooden enclosure and usually a small door.
Buttress	A structure built against a wall or building to give it stability.
Capital	The uppermost part of a column.
Cartouche	A French Renaissance motif, generally an oval tablet with ornamental scrollwork.
Chancel	The eastern part of a church occupied by the clergy and choir. Often separated from the rest of the church by an arch and screen.
Chantry chapel	A chapel usually attached to, or inside, a church, endowed for the celebration of masses for the soul of the founder.
Clerestory	The upper part of the nave wall, above the aisle roofs, perforated by a series of windows.
Corbel	A supporting projection of stone, wood, etc., on the face of a wall.
Crossing	The space at the intersection of the nave, chancel, and transepts.
Decorated	The second stage of English Gothic architecture from the end of the thirteenth-century to around 1350, characterised by elaborate ornamentation.
Early English	The earliest style of English Gothic, roughly covering the thirteenth-century and characterised by the use of pointed arches and narrow openings.
Fleur-de-lys	A heraldic device resembling three petals of an iris tied by an encircling band.
Floriated cross	A cross decorated with fleurs-de-lys.
Gargoyle	Rain-water spout, often in the form of a carved grotesque human or animal head, projecting from the gutter of a building.
Georgian	Period covering the reigns of the first four Georges, Kings of England (1714–1830).
Gothic	A style of architecture originating in France and spreading over western Europe from the twelfth to the sixteenth-century, characterised by a design emphasising skeletal construction, the great height of the buildings, and pointed arches.
Hammerbeam	A horizontal timber beam, which supports a wooden arch in a roof truss.
Lady chapel	A chapel dedicated to the Virgin Mary.
Lancet window	A tall, narrow window terminating in a pointed arch.
Lych gate	A roofed gate to a churchyard under which the bearers set down a bier to wait for the clergyman to escort them to the church.
Minster	Originally a church with a monastic foundation, but subsequently applied to many large churches.
Nave	The main body of the church occupied by the congregation, west of the chancel.
Norman	Denoting the period of architecture introduced from Normandy during the eleventh and twelfth-centuries, characterised by heavy walls, small windows, and open timber roofs.
Pediment	A low, triangular gable crowned with a projecting cornice, in the Greek, Roman, or Renaissance style.
Perpendicular	The last stage of English Gothic architecture roughly covering the period 1350–1550, in which a large proportion of the chief lines of the tracery intersect at right angles.
Piscina	A stone wall basin for washing the Communion vessels, with a drain so that the water used is passed onto the consecrated ground of the churchyard.
Quatrefoil	A decorative feature resembling a four-leaved clover.
Reredos	A decorative screen or decorative part of a wall behind and above an altar.
Reticulate	Netlike; covered with a network.
Rood	Cross or crucifix.
Rood screen	A screen, often of elaborate design, at the west end of the chancel, separating the chancel from the nave, and supporting a rood or crucifix.
Sacristy	A room in which the sacred vessels, vestments, etc., are kept.
Sarcophagus	A stone coffin, especially one bearing sculpture or inscriptions, often displayed as a monument.
Saxon	See *Anglo-Saxon*
Scratch dial	A sundial scratched onto the south wall of a church to mark the time of services.
Sedilia	Stone seats for the clergy, usually three, let into the south wall of the sanctuary.
Shaft	The part of a column or pillar between the base and the capital.
Squint	A small opening cut in the wall of a church, often in the chancel arch, to give a clear view of the altar.
Stoup	A basin for holy water near the entrance to a church.
Stringcourse	A horizontal band or course of stone, etc., projecting beyond or flush with the face of a building, often moulded and sometimes richly carved.
Tracery	Ornamental rib-work in the upper part of a window, screen or panel.
Transitional	Period of transition between Norman and Early English architecture: c. 1150–1200.
Trefoil	An ornamental feature resembling a three-leaved clover.
Triptych	A set of three panels side by side, bearing pictures, carvings, etc.
Tympanum	The area between the lintel of a doorway and the arch above.
Vault	An arched ceiling or roof, usually made of stone or brick.
Vesica	A pointed oval figure.

BIBLIOGRAPHY
(excluding church notes)

1. Bawden, William, trans., 'A Translation of the record called Domesday, so far as it relates to the County of York', London, 1809. (The Domesday survey was written in c. 1086 by order of William the Conqueror).
2. Betjeman, John, ed., 'Collins Pocket Guide to English Parish Churches. The North', London, 1968.
3. Brown, G. P., 'Four Sykes-Street Churches of the Great Wold Valley: Kirby Grindalythe, St. Andrew; West Lutton, St. Mary; Helperthorpe, St. Peter; Weaverthorpe, St. Andrew', 1983.
4. Camden, William, 'Britannia', ed. and trans. by Edmund Gibson, London, 1695. (Camden's 'Britannia' was first published in 1586).
5. Carter, Robert A., 'A Visitor's Guide to Yorkshire Churches', Bradford, 1976.
6. Christie, Graham, 'Some notes on the history of Pocklington church', Pocklington, 1974.
7. Duke, Donald, 'A History of All Saints, Nafferton', in press.
8. Hawkins, D. S., 'The Parish Church of St. Martin, Burton Agnes. The Church of Dark Knights and Gospel Lights', in press.
9. Hutchinson, John, 'George Edmund Street in East Yorkshire. A Centenary Exhibition', University of Hull, 1981.
10. Mann, Faith, 'Early Mediaeval Church Sculpture: A Study of 12th Century Fragments in East Yorkshire,' Hutton Press, 1985.
11. Mee, Arthur, 'The King's England. Yorkshire – East Riding', (fully revised and edited by C. L. S. Linnell), 1964 (first published in 1941).
12. Taylor, H. M. and Taylor, Joan, 'Anglo-Saxon Architecture', Vol. II, Cambridge, 1965.
13. Wright, Geoffrey N., 'Yorkshire. The East Riding', London, 1976.